Maïte Roche

First prayers
for little children

 CTS Children's Books

Maïte Roche

First prayers
for little children

In the name of the Father,
and of the Son,
and of the Holy Spirit. Amen.

Our Father,
who art in heaven,
hallowed be thy name.
Thy kingdom come.
Thy will be done on earth,
as it is in heaven.
Give us this day
our daily bread,
and forgive us our trespasses
as we forgive those who
trespass against us,
and lead us not into
temptation but deliver
us from evil.

Amen.

In the name of the Father,
and of the Son,
and of the Holy Spirit.
Amen.

Hail Mary,
full of grace,
the Lord is with thee.
Blessed art thou
among women,
and blessed is the fruit
of thy womb, Jesus.
Holy Mary, Mother of God,
pray for us sinners, now
and at the hour of our death.

Amen.

In the name of the Father,
and of the Son,
and of the Holy Spirit.
Amen.

Thank you, Lord,
for this lovely day.
I pray to you for my
Mummy and Daddy,
my family, my friends
and everyone I have met today.
I come to you with my
joys and sorrows,
I offer you all the treasures
of my heart.

Amen.

 In the name of the Father,
and of the Son,
and of the Holy Spirit.
Amen.

Dear Mary,
watch over me with love.
Open my heart
to welcome Jesus.
Help me to grow,
and to do what is right,
today and every day.

Amen.

In the name of the Father,
and of the Son,
and of the Holy Spirit.
Amen.

Dear God,
you know me by my name.
You love me like a father.
I am your child.
Help me to grow, staying
close to you, every day.
Alleluia! Alleluia!

Amen.

 In the name of the Father,
and of the Son,
and of the Holy Spirit.
Amen.

With you, Mary,
I say thank you for Jesus.
With you, Mary,
I sing out my happiness:
"The Lord has done
marvellous things for me!
Holy is his Name!"

Amen.

In the name of the Father,
and of the Son,
and of the Holy Spirit.
Amen.

Jesus, I love you.
Come into my house
and it will become
your house.

Amen.

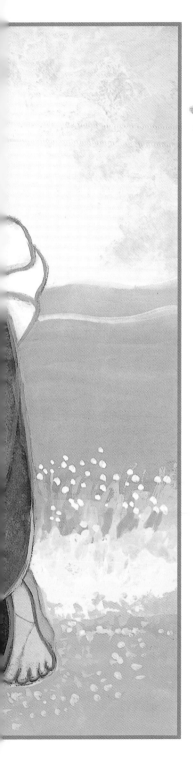

In the name of the Father,
and of the Son,
and of the Holy Spirit.
Amen.

Mary,
help me,
cheer me up.
I come to you with my
sorrow,
and I trust in you.
You understand me,
and you love me.

Amen.

In the name of the Father,
and of the Son,
and of the Holy Spirit.
Amen.

Jesus,
you are my friend:
When I'm feeling sad,
please cheer me up.
When I'm feeling happy,
share my happiness.
When I'm asleep,
watch over me.

Amen.

In the name of the Father,
and of the Son,
and of the Holy Spirit.
Amen.

Jesus, Mary and Joseph,
God's Holy Family,
pray for us.
Protect my Mummy and Daddy,
and all the families
in the world.
Help us to make peace
so we can live in God's Love.

Amen.

In the name of the Father,
and of the Son,
and of the Holy Spirit.
Amen.

Jesus, give us
your Spirit of Love.
Help us to be peacemakers.
Teach us to love each other
as you love us,
and bring us together
in the joy of God
our Father.

Amen.

In the name of the Father,
and of the Son,
and of the Holy Spirit.
Amen.

Mary, hear our prayer,
and, like a mother,
welcome all the people
who come to you.
Give courage to
those who are ill,
give happiness to those
who are crying,
protect the littlest ones,
and lead us to Jesus
our Saviour.

Amen.

Goodnight, Jesus;
goodnight, Mary;
goodnight, all God's Saints;
goodnight, my Guardian
Angel.
Watch over me
and everyone I love,
every day and every night.

Amen.

Goodnight, Mary;
I entrust to you
everyone I love.
I will go to sleep in peace.
Watch over me,
and hold me
in the Love of God.

Amen.

CTS Children's Books

The Bible for little children, *by Maïte Roche*
(ISBN 1 86082 399 8 CTS Code CH 2)

The Gospel for little children, *by Maïte Roche*
(ISBN 1 86082 400 5 CTS Code CH 1)

The Rosary, *by Juliette Levivier*
(ISBN 1 86082 397 1 CTS Code CH 3)

The Way of the Cross, *by Juliette Levivier*
(ISBN 1 86082 398 X CTS Code CH 4)

First prayers for little children, *by Maïte Roche*
(ISBN 978 1 86082 443 2 CTS Code CH 5)

Praying with the friends of Jesus, *by Juliette Levivier*
(ISBN 978 1 86082 444 9 CTS Code CH 6)

Prayers around the Crib, *by Juliette Levivier*
(ISBN 978 1 86082 445 6 CTS Code CH 7)

The most beautiful Christmas Story, *by Maïte Roche*
(ISBN 978 1 86082 446 3 CTS Code CH 8)

Faith for children, *by Christine Pedotti*
(ISBN 978 1 86082 447 0 CTS Code CH 9)

First prayers for little children: Published 2007 by the Incorporated Catholic Truth Society, 40-46 Harleyford Road, London SE11 5AY. Tel: 020 7640 0042; Fax: 020 7640 0046; www.cts-online.org.uk. Copyright © 2007 The Incorporated Catholic Truth Society in this English-language edition.

ISBN: 978 1 86082 443 2   CTS Code CH 5

Compiled from two sources **Premières prières avec Marie** and **Premières prières pour tous les soirs** written and illustrated by Maïte Roche, published 2006 by Edifa-Mame, 15-27 rue Moussorgski, 75018 Paris; **Premières prières avec Marie** ISBN: 978-2-7289-1150-9; **Premières prières pour tous les soirs** ISBN: 978-2-7289-1151-6; Copyright © Groupe Fleurus 2006.